JON JONES

Jon Jones elbows Dominick Reyes at UFC 247.

JON JONES

ODYSSEYS

MICHAEL E. GOODMAN

CREATIVE EDUCATION · CREATIVE PAPERBACKS

Published by Creative Education and Creative Paperbacks
P.O. Box 227, Mankato, Minnesota 56002
Creative Education and Creative Paperbacks
are imprints of The Creative Company
www.thecreativecompany.us

Copyright © 2025 Creative Education, Creative Paperbacks
International copyright reserved in all countries.
No part of this book may be reproduced in any form
without written permission from the publisher.

Design by Graham Morgan
Art direction by Tom Morgan
Edited by Kremena Spengler

Images by Associated Press/John Locher, cover; Getty Images/
Al Bello, 8, 12, 30, 34-35, Chris Unger, 46, Christian Petersen, 60,
Ethan Miller, 49, Jeff Bottari, 69, 70-71, 75, Jim Kemper, 16, Josh
Hedges, 2, 4-5, 15, 24, 51, 63, Mike Roach, 6, Rob Carr, 20, Sean M. Haffey, 64;
Unsplash/Nathan Dumlao, 59; Wikimedia Commons/Andrius Petrucenia, 39,
Bjoertvedt, 11, Evilarry, 19, Krystof Gauthier (France), 26, public domain, 56,
Tony Webster, 52

Library of Congress Cataloging-in-Publication Data
Names: Goodman, Michael E., author.
Title: Jon Jones / by Michael E. Goodman.
Description: Mankato, Minnesota : Creative Education and Creative
   Paperbacks, [2025] | Series: Odysseys in extreme sports | ATOS 7 |
   Includes bibliographical references and index. | Audience: Ages 12-15
   years | Audience: Grades 7-9 | Summary: "Step into the Octagon with
   mixed martial arts (MMA) fighter Jon Jones. Witness triumphs,
   challenges, and risks in his extreme sports title for high school
   readers. Includes action photos, a glossary, index, and further
   resources"– Provided by publisher.
Identifiers: LCCN 2024025238 (print) | LCCN 2024025239 (ebook) |
   ISBN 9798889893127 (lib. bdg.) | ISBN 9781682776780 (paperback) |
   ISBN 9798889894230 (ebook)
Subjects: LCSH: Jones, Jon (Jonathan Dwight), 1987- Juvenile literature. |
   Mixed martial arts–New York–Biography—Juvenile literature. | Ultimate
   Fighting Championship (Organization)—Juvenile literature.
Classification: LCC GV1113.J66 G66 2025 (print) | LCC GV1113.J66 (ebook)
   | DDC 796.81092 [B]-dc23/eng/20240712
LC record available at https://lccn.loc.gov/2024025238
LC ebook record available at https://lccn.loc.gov/2024025239

Printed in China

Jon Jones kicks Dominick Reyes during the light heavyweight championship fight at UFC 247 on February 8, 2020, in Houston, Texas.

Jon Jones poses for a portrait during a UFC photo session on February 5, 2020, in Houston, Texas.

CONTENTS

Introduction 9

Building a Champion 17

   The Jones Siblings 20

   12-to-6 Elbow 26

Earning and Keeping the Belt 31

   The UFC Belt 39

   Early Stoppage 43

Criticism and Controversy 44

   Bitter Rivals 51

   What's a 'No Contest'? 56

A Triumphant Return 61

   3-2-1 70

Selected Bibliography 76

Glossary 77

Websites 79

Index 80

Introduction

On March 19, 2011, 23-year-old Jon "Bones" Jones took on 29-year-old Brazilian champion Mauricio "Shogun" Rua for the Ultimate Fighting Championship (UFC) **light heavyweight** title in Newark, New Jersey. The two fighters were headlining a 12-bout **card** as part of UFC 128. (The UFC numbers each of its fight-night events consecutively.) More than 12,600 fans attended UFC 128 in person at the Prudential Center in Newark, New Jersey, while more than 445,000 had purchased **pay-per-view** passes to see the full card remotely.

OPPOSITE: Jon Jones punches Mauricio "Shogun" Rua during the light heavyweight championship fight at UFC 128 on March 19, 2011, in Newark, New Jersey.

Building a Champion

Jonathan Dwight Jones was born in Rochester, New York, on July 19, 1987. He was the third of four children, three boys and a girl. All of the boys were tall and athletic, and all started out as high-school football players at Union-Endicott High School in Endicott, New York. Jon's brothers, Arthur and Chandler, stayed with football into college at Syracuse University and were high draft picks into the National Football League (NFL) after college.

OPPOSITE: Jon Jones in 2009

Jon Jones (left) and his brother Arthur (right)

The Jones Siblings

Jon Jones comes from a large family, not so much in terms of number of members but in terms of size. His two brothers were both standouts in college football and played in the National Football League (NFL). In his days as a defensive lineman, his older brother Arthur was 6-foot-3 and weighed 301 pounds. He retired from the NFL in 2017. Younger brother Chandler, a 6-foot-5 and 265-pound edge rusher, played for New England, Arizona, and Las Vegas in the NFL. He has a Super Bowl ring and played in four Pro Bowl games. Jones also had a sister, Carmen, who died of cancer at age 17.

all by TKOs or by opponents' submissions. His success got the attention of the leaders of the UFC, who signed Jones to a four-fight deal. At the time, he became the youngest fighter in the UFC ranks.

Jones got off to a quick start in the UFC, winning his first two bouts handily with a variety of unusual moves, such as spinning elbows and a spinning back kick. In his third fight, he introduced a new weapon to his arsenal—a guillotine choke, a Brazilian jiujitsu move in which a fighter uses his arms to encircle an opponent's neck from the front and applies pressure to make breathing difficult. Not surprisingly, Jones's opponent in that third match, Jake O'Brien, **tapped out** when Bones applied the chokehold during the second round of their bout.

Jones was riding high as he next faced off against fellow light heavyweight Matt Hamill in an event publi-

Jones hits Vera with a left elbow, 2010.

heavyweight Brandon Vera, Jones stormed to the middle of the Octagon and quickly took Vera down to the mat. The two grappled, and Vera drilled Jones with an illegal kick to the head, earning a point deduction from the referee. When the fight resumed, Jones stunned Vera with a left elbow to the jaw. The elbow caused Vera to turn his head for a split second, and Jones began showering him with blows. The fight was over seconds later, as the referee stepped in and awarded Jones the victory via TKO.

After Jones won his next two bouts with little trouble, he was promised a "huge step-up in competition" by UFC President Dana White. "Jones is the real deal, and he just catapulted himself into the top eight in the world," White told reporters. "He's got to keep his head together, stay focused, and keep doing all the right things

12-to-6 Elbow

Defined as striking directly downwards from overhead using the point of the elbow, 12-to-6 elbow strikes are illegal under the Unified Rules of Mixed Martial Arts. The MMA rules were developed by a New Jersey athletic commission in the 1990s to make sure that fighters in venues all around the country follow the same rules of sportsmanship and safety. Commission members had seen karate demonstrations where athletes broke thick boards and cement blocks with 12-to-6 elbows. They feared that, if used in the heat of a bout, the move could lead to serious injuries. All other elbow strikes are allowed under the rules.

in training. This kid is going to do very well. He's going to make a lot of money."

Jones agreed with White's assessment and was eager to have a shot at the light heavyweight championship. That chance came in March 2011, thanks, in part, to an unfortunate accident. Jones's friend and training partner Rashad Evans was scheduled to take on Mauricio "Shogun" Rua for the light heavyweight title. But Evans suffered a knee injury in training and was forced to back out of the match. The decision was made to put Jones up against Rua for the title a month later as part of UFC 128. Ticket sales took off for the bout, and Jones began serious training to prepare for the fight.

What Jones could never have imagined was that the bout against Rua would actually be his second major confrontation on fight day. Several hours before UFC 128 was scheduled to begin, Jones and his two coaches drove through Paterson, New Jersey. They were looking for a famous waterfall where they planned to hold a meditation session to help Jones get into the proper mental focus for the fight. They had been told that the area was peaceful, but it was also a place where muggings sometimes occurred. Suddenly, an elderly couple ran by them. The couple were shouting that someone had stopped their car and had run off with their belongings. Jones and one of his coaches immediately went into action, chasing down the mugger and quickly catching up to him. "I'm closing in on the guy, and I see him starting to get winded," Jones related to a reporter for the online newspaper *The Mirror US*. "The guy looks back and trips over his own foot. When he tried to stand up, I kind of kicked his ankle out. My coach came out of nowhere and jumped on the guy's back. I grabbed the guy's feet and figure-foured his legs [bent them into a pretzel]. We held him until the police came. It was great. Me and my coaches then all felt like superheroes."

The bout against Shogun went almost as well for Jones. He dominated the first two rounds of the scheduled five-round championship fight and quickly took out his opponent midway through round three, earning the victory via TKO. Less than three years after joining the UFC as a 21-year-old rookie and after only eight fights, Jones was the organization's youngest champion ever.

Earning and Keeping the Belt

Immediately after being declared the winner over Mauricio "Shogun" Rua in UFC 128, Jon "Bones" Jones was presented with a gold-and-jewel-studded belt proclaiming him a UFC World Champion. He proudly buckled the belt around his waist as he acknowledged the cheers from the crowd. He was determined to hold onto the belt as long as possible by successfully defending his crown against other high-ranked opponents in his weight class.

OPPOSITE: Jon Jones prepares to deliver an elbow strike against Mauricio "Shogun" Rua during the light heavyweight championship.

And that is just what he did. Between September 2011 and January 2015, Jones defeated eight different challengers in title bouts. He recorded three victories by submission, one by TKO, and four by unanimous decisions from the judges. Jones trained carefully for each bout. He knew he would face serious competition. In his first four title defenses after defeating Rua, Jones took on four other former UFC champions. In September 2011, he forced Quinton "Rampage" Jackson to submit in the fourth round. Jackson had won two light heavyweight title bouts in 2007. In April 2012, Jones forced Brazilian karate expert Lyoto "The Dragon" Machida to tap out in the second round of their title fight. Machida had been a UFC champion a few years earlier when he defeated Shogun Rua. Then he had lost the title to Rua in their return match. Not long after that, Jones had beaten Rua in their championship bout.

"BETWEEN SEPTEMBER 2011 AND JANUARY 2015, JONES DEFEATED EIGHT DIFFERENT CHALLENGERS IN TITLE BOUTS."

Jones's next title defense in September 2012 was a battle of old friends. He faced off against his former training partner Rashad Evans. Evans had been a wrestling star at Michigan State University before turning to MMA and then joining the UFC. Evans and Jones had first connected at the Jackson Wink MMA Academy

Jon Jones (*left*) fights Rashad Evans (*right*) during the light heavyweight title bout at UFC 145 on April 21, 2012, in Atlanta, Georgia.

in Albuquerque, New Mexico, where both trained. "I remember when he first came to Jackson's, and I watched him workout, I was like, man, now I have somebody I can play with," Evans recalled. "We'd go back and forth, drilling and having fun."

In their training sessions, the two fighters tried out new moves and holds and learned from each other. It was evident in their title match that Jones and Evans each knew what to expect from his opponent. The fight went back and forth, though Jones was the more aggressive and kept racking up points on the judges' scorecards. The bout went the full five rounds and ended in a unanimous decision for Jones.

Jones's fourth defense came against Vitor Belfort, a lefty Brazilian fighter who was more than 10 years older than Jones. Belfort had been a UFC champion in 2004 but was no longer in Jones's class, or so most fans thought. Belfort put a scare into Jones when he got the younger man into a devastating **armbar** that clearly caused some pain. Fans held their breath, worried that Jones might tap out. But he managed to fight his way out of the hold and took back control of the fight. In the end, Belfort was forced to submit early in the fourth round, and Jones held onto his belt.

There was more drama in Jones's next title defense in April 2013 against Chael Sonnen, who had been an all-American college wrestler before turning to MMA.

Jones came out aggressively to start the match—perhaps too aggressively. Somehow, he managed to dislocate a toe while pursuing Sonnen in the Octagon. The toe was hanging from his bare foot at an awkward angle. Jones ignored the pain and went right at Sonnen, taking control of the action and prompting the referee to stop the fight and award the win to Jones by TKO just 27 seconds before the end of round one. The timing was lucky. Had the bell rung to end the round, the referee, seeing the state of Jones's toe, might have been forced to stop the fight and declare Sonnen the winner instead.

When Jones defeated Swedish fighter Alexander Gustafsson by unanimous decision in UFC 165 (September 2013), it was his sixth title defense in a row, a new UFC record for light heavyweights. He would add to that record with unanimous-decision victories over

The UFC Belt

A UFC belt is a very special prize. In the early days of competition, champions received a new belt with each successful defense. That was when the metal parts on the belt were gold-plated and not solid gold, as they are now. Today, with each belt valued at more than $300,000, giving out a new belt to the same fighter after each title bout would be very expensive. So when a champion successfully defends his or her crown, an additional precious stone is added to the original belt. Thus the belt gets more valuable with each successful defense.

Jones was stripped of his light heavyweight title and suspended indefinitely.

The suspension was lifted after six months, and the UFC reinstated Jones to its active roster. Why was the suspension raised so quickly? No one at the UFC explained. But Jones was a big draw at the box office and had a growing fan base. Those might be some of the reasons.

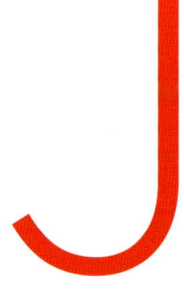ones finally got back into the Octagon in April 2016, 15 months after his last title fight. He scored a unanimous

Early Stoppage

An early stoppage occurs when a referee intervenes to halt a fight before all scheduled rounds have been concluded. Referees step in when they believe fighters are unable to defend themselves effectively, when fighters are unwilling to engage in further combat, when they have been subjected to numerous potentially damaging strikes without offering adequate resistance, or when a fighter's physical condition is seriously compromised. Early stoppages are controversial. MMA competitors often feel that, given a brief time to recover, they could successfully get back into and win a fight. But a referee's decision cannot be challenged.

decision over Haitian **striker** Ovince Saint Preux and was awarded an interim light heavyweight belt. (No permanent champion had been determined yet.) But Jones's return to the top would be short-lived. He would get involved in more controversy and face additional punishments over the next few years as he tried to turn his life around and become a champion again.

JON JONES

Criticism and Controversy

In his book *Jon Jones: Outside the Cage*, MMA fan and author H. Walniel noted: "Throughout his professional career, Jon Jones has clearly inspired both admiration and hate. We all have our personal and professional opinion of him, as a fighter and a human being; his behavior inside and outside the cage does that to us… On the one hand, we admire his rise to the UFC light heavyweight title and his impressive fighting skills. On the other hand, some people hate him for his lack of honesty and sportsmanship."

Jones is particularly sensitive to claims that he has displayed poor sportsmanship in the Octagon. Some fighters and sports commentators have accused Jones of purposely or accidentally poking his opponents in the eye during bouts. That is against the UFC's Code of Conduct. An example occurred in his April 2014 win over Grover Teixeira. Jones was criticized for fighting with an open hand during the bout, leading to his poking Teixeira in the eye. In an interview streamed on YouTube's The MMA Hour after the fight, Jones said, "I realize I do it. It's not on purpose. If you watch my fights, a lot of times when guys get poked in the eyes, it's me extending my arm in a reactionary way. I do put a hand on people's foreheads to maintain distance. That's what you saw in the Teixeira fight. But to say I am purposely poking people in the eye, it's just inaccurate." (Jones's

Jon Jones lands an illegal knee against Anthony Smith in their light heavyweight championship bout.

huge seven-foot wingspan may support his contention that some eye pokes have resulted from just extending his long arms.)

FC veteran Bas Rutten responded harshly to Jones's comments and called him "a dirty fighter." Jones disagreed but promised to change. "I don't believe it's dirty," Jones said. "It's something that I do instinctually, but it is something that I need to work on."

As for criticism of the fighter's honesty, H. Walniel points to a number of Jones's actions outside the cage in which he has shown poor judgment or bad behavior. He has been arrested several times for driving under the influence of alcohol or drugs (DUI). These arrests resulted in his being ordered to pay fines and to perform hours of community service. He has also failed tests for use of banned substances, such as **anabolic steroids**. These lapses led to his being suspended by the UFC on two occasions and having his title removed twice.

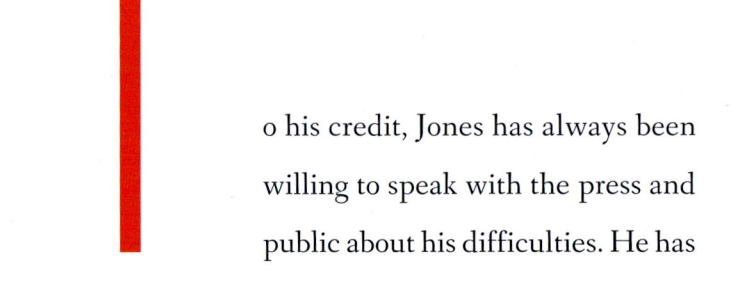

To his credit, Jones has always been willing to speak with the press and public about his difficulties. He has

Jon Jones at a news conference to address his potential violation of the UFC's drug policy

never gone into hiding or refused to be interviewed. However, he has not always recognized the gravity of his actions. After his first DUI arrest in May 2012, when he had driven his expensive car into a telephone pole in Binghamton, New York, Jones apologized to fans for his poor judgment but also hoped they would have "short memories." He believed the DUI arrest would set him free in some ways. Now people would not expect him always to be perfect. They would see that he was "a 25-year-old guy that does dumb stuff."

Jones admitted that he has learned some important lessons from the situation. "Things could have gone wrong. I could have hurt someone; I could not be sitting here right now. I could be dead, and I'm blessed that that didn't happen. So to go through such struggle and have many people

Bitter Rivals

The rivalry between Jon Jones and Daniel Cormier started in 2010, when Jones walked up to Cormier and said, "I bet I can take you down." Jones said he was just trying to be friendly, but Cormier saw his words as an insult. They met again at a press conference before a scheduled 2014 bout and almost got into a brawl. When they finally fought in 2015, they spent much of the tight match bad-mouthing each other. Jones taunted Cormier, and Cormier screamed insults because of Jones's problems outside the Octagon. Jones won that fight by unanimous decision and earned a "No Contest" ruling for their second bout in July 2017.

Jones apologized to fans for his poor judgment after a DUI arrest.

criticizing me, it's all been a blessing. It's another opportunity for me to grow as a man."

For Walniel and other critics, Jones's getting caught using cocaine before his January 2015 fight against Daniel Cormier was another black mark. He was forced to pay a hefty fine by the UFC. Once again, Jones took responsibility for his actions, saying that cocaine was not "his thing" and that he had messed up. He apologized to his fans and to the UFC and said he was ready to get his life back in order and to begin preparing for his next fight.

What's a 'No Contest'?

Jon Jones's 2017 bout with Daniel Cormier ended in a "No Contest" decision. In other words, he neither won nor lost that fight. A No Contest is usually the result of something that happens outside the control of one or both fighters. For example, if one fighter gets accidentally poked in the eye, it could force the fighter to withdraw with neither competitor having actually won. In Jones's case, the state commissioners turned his TKO victory over Cormier into a No Contest when they were unsure if Jones had actually taken illegal substances before the fight or if they were still in his system from some time before.

scheduled rematch with Daniel Cormier on suspicion of taking performance-enhancing substances. The incident really upset Jones. During a tearful press conference, the former champion appealed the decision by the U.S. Anti-Doping Agency (USADA). "Being labeled as a cheat hurts me more than anything else I've been through in my career," he said.

The agency later revealed that the substances for which Jones tested positive had been unknowingly included in a legal medication that the fighter was taking. The ban was lifted, and the bout with Cormier was rescheduled

"THE FIGHTER ASSURED FANS THAT HIS LEGAL PROBLEMS WERE OVER AND THAT HE WAS PLANNING TO PUT HIS FOCUS ENTIRELY ON COMBAT INSIDE THE OCTAGON."

for July 29, 2017. Jones won that fight in a third-round knockout for his 28th UFC victory, but post-fight testing revealed an anabolic steroid in his system once again. Was this a new substance, or one left over in his system from a previous test? State sports commissioners could not be certain. Nevertheless, they decided that Jones's win should be replaced with a "No Contest" ruling and that Cormier should be reinstated as light heavyweight champion. Jones was also given a 15-month suspension. After all of the controversy, Jones's record continued to show only one loss—the disqualification for illegal

> Jones wanted to put his legal troubles behind him and put all his efforts towards training and fighting.

punches in his 2009 bout against Matt Hamill—and now one "No Contest" to go along with 27 wins. The fighter assured fans that his legal problems were over and that he was planning to put his focus entirely on combat inside the Octagon.

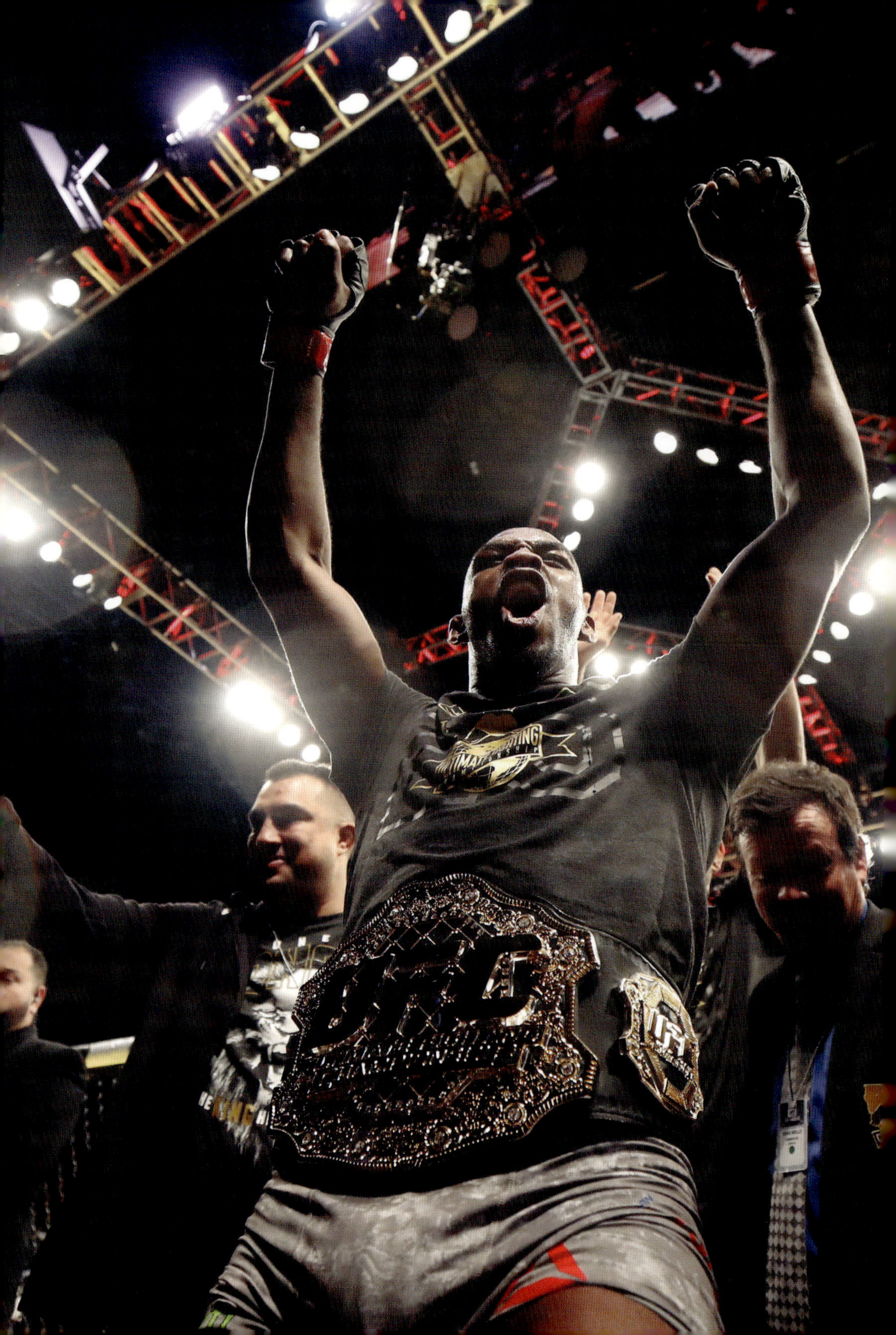
UFC

JON JONES

A Triumphant Return

With his suspension ending, Jones was scheduled to return to the Octagon on December 29, 2018, in Los Angeles, California, to fight a rematch with Alexander Gustafsson. The winner would be crowned UFC light heavyweight champion. At a news conference at Madison Square Garden in New York a month before the bout, the two fighters squared off for publicity photos.

OPPOSITE: Jon Jones celebrates after defeating Alexander Gustafsson of Sweden in the light heavyweight fight at UFC 232 on December 29, 2018, in Los Angeles, California.

Jones pushed Gustafsson, which his Swedish opponent didn't appreciate. Jones explained his action to ESPN reporters: "I was thinking, 'We're in New York; let's give the fans some excitement.'"

The bout itself turned out to be less exciting than the press conference. Jones dominated the fight, which ended in a third-round TKO. After Jones successfully passed all post-fight drug tests, he was once again awarded a championship belt. The UFC announced that Jones would next defend his title in March 2019 in Las Vegas, Nevada, against Anthony Smith. In the meantime, he had to pass more drug tests. "I'm O.K. with it. I've got nothing to hide," the fighter said. All tests leading up to the bout proved negative, so the fight was a go.

Jones had little trouble gaining a unanimous decision over Smith, though there was one scary moment in round

Jon Jones kicks Alexander Gustafsson in their UFC light heavyweight championship.

Jones blocks a punch from Santos.

four. Jones had taken Smith down to the mat and, in the heat of the action, landed a knee into the face of his fallen opponent. The referee stopped the fight momentarily and deducted two points for the illegal move. It might have been worse for Jones if Smith had not been able to continue. In that case, Jones might have been disqualified, and Smith might have been declared champion.

Jones's next fight proved even scarier for the champ. Thiago Santos, a powerful Brazilian striker, matched him blow for blow throughout all five rounds. In the end, two judges ruled in Jones's favor, and one ruled for Santos. It was Jones's first title defense to result in a split decision.

Jones had another close call in his next bout in February 2020 against previously undefeated Californian Dominick Reyes. He was able to retain his title, but fans watching the bout live in Houston, Texas, and at pay-

Fans were not sure what to expect from Jones in a heavyweight title bout against Gane. After all, Jones had not fought in the Octagon since he beat Reyes in their controversial battle in February 2020. And several of his light heavyweight title bouts before that had been tight struggles. Was Jones slowing down or easing up too much to make the transition successfully to heavyweight champ? Fans and critics alike had their answer just more than two minutes into the Jones–Gane fight.

The contest got off to a rocky start when Gane kicked Jones squarely in the groin in the opening seconds and received a warning from the referee. Jones shook off the pain and began moving in on Gane. They traded light punches and feints. Then, Jones found an opening. He ducked a punch and came up behind Gane, taking him down to the mat and up against the cage. Gane, who was used to

Jones gained significant weight with the goal of becoming a heavyweight champion.

3-2-1

When Jon Jones forced heavyweight champ Ciryl Gane to submit in just 2 minutes and 4 seconds, it was actually the third-shortest UFC heavyweight title bout of all time. In UFC 51 in February 2005, Andrei Arlovski from Belarus submitted 6-foot-8 Tim Sylvia in just 47 seconds with a powerful right-hand punch followed by a heel twist. Arlovski said it wasn't an easy win. After all, he had trained hard for the fight for three months before entering the Octagon. Amazingly, Sylvia had also been taken out in just 51 seconds in a title fight two years before, when Frank Mir broke his arm with a punishing armbar.

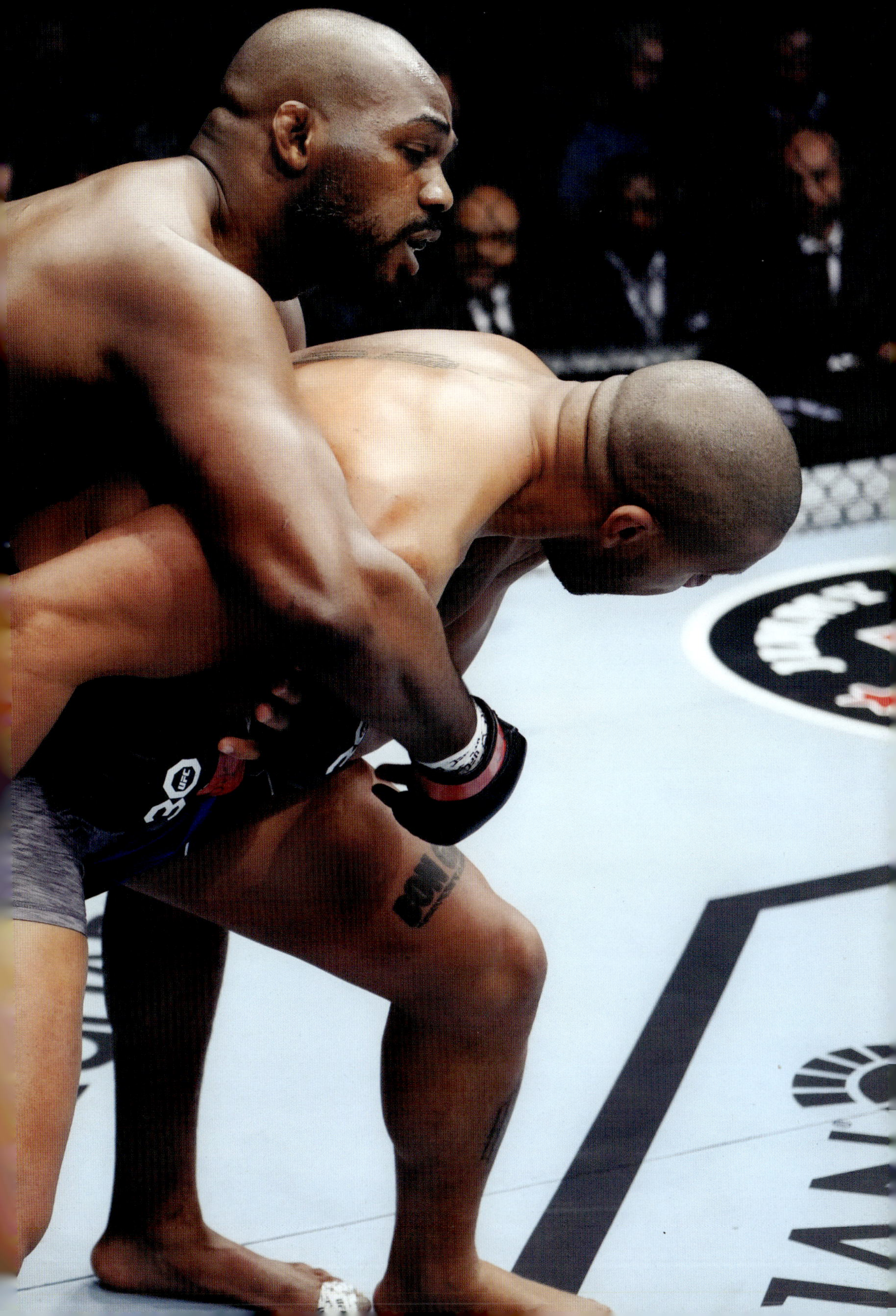

battling slower-moving heavyweight fighters, was clearly uncomfortable grappling on the mat with his speedy and powerful opponent. Jones began pounding Gane's body with short, hard punches. Then he got his arms around Gane's neck and began tightening a guillotine choke. Gane couldn't escape. And he could barely breathe. Slowly, he put his hand on Jones's shoulder and tapped twice, ending the fight. It was 2 minutes, 4 seconds into round one. After the fight, one commentor on Twitter wrote that the ring announcer had taken longer to introduce the two fighters than Jones had taken to defeat his opponent.

After the referee elevated Jones's arm to signify his victory, Jones danced around the Octagon, waved to his king-sized father and brothers who were at the fight, and received a big hug and kiss from his fiancée Jessie Moses. Talking above the pandemonium, the pay-per-view announcer Jon Anik could be heard shouting: "There is no denying Jon Jones now. He is the number one of all time!"

Jones hoped to defend his new title before the end of 2023, but the plans were delayed several times because of surgeries he needed, to take care of injuries to a hand and a pectoral muscle. A fight later in 2024 was still in the planning.

Jon Jones certainly has the credentials to be considered the UFC GOAT. He successfully defended his light heavyweight title 11 times, including 8 times in a row.

No other competitor has come close to those achievements. Jones reigned as champion for 2,042 days, the third longest in UFC history (behind Anderson Silva and Demetrious Johnson). When Jones defeated Gane for the heavyweight title in March 2023, he became one of only a handful of UFC fighters who have held the championship in more than one weight class. There is no denying his greatness as a fighter, but is he a great champion when his actions outside of the Octagon are taken into consideration? That is still to be determined.

Jon Jones enters the Octagon for the heavyweight championship fight at UFC 285.

Selected Bibliography

Cerdá, Carlos Martinez and Victor Martinez Cerdá. *101 Strange But True UFC Facts*. Self-published; Sold by Amazon.com Services LLC, 2022.

Coral, Barry. "Jon Jones is two-weight UFC champion after demolishing Ciryl Gane in one round." *BBC Sport*, March 5, 2023, https://www.bbc.com/sport/mixed-martial-arts/64852894.

Gerbasi, Thomas. *UFC Encyclopedia*. New York: DK, 2011.

Okonkwo, Gerald. *The Return of Jon Jones to the UFC*. Kindle Edition. Self-published; Sold by Amazon.com Services LLC, 2023.

Wagenheim, Jeff. "Jon Jones' Complicated Legacy of MMA Greatest and Personal Troubles." ESPN, March 5, 2023, https://www.espn.com/mma/story/_/id/25608180/jon-jones-complicated-legacy-mma-greatness-personal-trouble.

Wagenheim, Jeff. "Winning is Everything: The Evolution of Jon Jones." *ESPN*, February 4, 2020, https://www.espn.com/mma/story/_/id/28628166/winning-everything-evolution-jon-jones-ahead-ufc-247.

Walniel H., *Jon Jones: Outside the Cage*. Self-published; Sold by Amazon.com Services LLC, 2017.

Glossary

anabolic steroids   drugs related to male hormones, used by athletes to increase muscle size, strength, and performance. They are banned by most sports organizations.

armbar   a move in which a fighter straightens an opponent's arm out, then forces it beyond its normal range at the elbow

card   in sports, a list of the matches taking place in a combat-sport event, including the main event and undercard bouts

flying knee   a martial arts knee kick performed in stand-up fighting by rushing toward and jumping into the opponent

heavyweight   in MMA, a fighter who weighs 206 to 265 pounds (93 to 120 kg)

light heavyweight   in MMA, a fighter who weighs 186 to 205 pounds (84 to 93 kg)

Octagon	the eight-sided raised platform surrounded by fencing that is used for UFC fights. The angles are wider than a square, preventing fighters from getting trapped.
own recognizance	release, without having to post bail, if a defendant promises to appear when required to do so
pay-per-view	cable television service in which subscribers pay to watch a particular event
striker	an MMA fighter who prefers to attack from a standing position using kicks, punches, knees, or elbows to subdue an opponent
submission	when a fighter gives up in a match; often signaled by tapping the floor or opponent with the hand or foot or by calling out to the judge
tap out	indicate submission, often by tapping the floor or an opponent to stop a fight
technical knockout (TKO)	stopping a match when a referee determines that a fighter's opponent is unable to continue

Websites

How the Ultimate Fighting Championship Works
https://entertainment.howstuffworks.com/ufc1.htm
This overview of UFC includes basic information, fighting techniques, a brief history, a look at the future, and numerous links for additional information.

The Official Home of Ultimate Fighting Championship
http://www.ufc.com
The official UFC website includes news, fighter biographies, previews of upcoming fights, results, photos and videos, merchandise, and more.

Index

Albuquerque, New Mexico, 36, 41, 54
anabolic steroids, 48, 58
Cormier, Daniel, 40, 51, 53, 56, 57, 58
Evans, Rashad, 27, 33, 35, 36
football, 17, 18, 20
Gane, Ciryl, 67, 68, 70, 72, 74
guillotine choke, 21, 72
Gustafsson, Alexander, 38, 61, 62, 63
Hamill, Matt, 21, 22, 23, 59
Jones, Arthur, 17, 20
Jones, Chandler, 17, 20
mixed martial arts (MMA), 18, 26, 33, 37, 43, 44, 45
Moses, Jessie, 72
Ngannou, Francis, 66, 67
Rua, Mauricio "Shogun," 9, 10, 13, 27, 29, 30, 31, 32
Sonnen, Chael, 37, 38
Sylvia, Tim, 70
Teixeira, Grover, 40, 45
UFC belt, 31, 39
UFC's Athlete Code of Conduct, 41, 45
Ultimate Fighting Championship (UFC), 9, 13, 14, 15, 21, 23, 25, 27, 29, 31, 32, 33, 37, 38, 39, 41, 42, 44, 45, 48, 53, 54, 55, 58, 61, 62, 63, 66, 67, 70, 73, 74
USADA (U.S. Anti-Doping Agency), 57
Vera, Brandon, 24, 25
Walniel, H., 44, 47, 53
White, Dana, 25, 27, 67
wrestling, 10, 18, 22, 33